bold colours

Sarah Lynch

BONNIER BOOKS

BONNIER BOOKS

This edition published by Bonnier Books,
Appledram Barns, Birdham Road, Chichester,
West Sussex PO20 7 EQ, UK
www.bonnierbooks.co.uk

WELDON OWEN GROUP
Chief Executive Officer **John Owen**
Chief Financial Officer **Simon Fraser**

WELDON OWEN INC.
Chief Executive Officer and President **Terry Newell**
Senior VP, International Sales **Stuart Laurence**
VP, Sales and Marketing **Amy Kaneko**

VP, Creative Director **Gaye Allen**
Senior Art Director **Emma Boys**
Designers **Anna Giladi** and **Diana Heom**

VP, Publisher **Roger Shaw**
Executive Editor **Elizabeth Dougherty**
Managing Editor **Karen Templer**
Project Editor **Veronica Peterson**
Editorial Assistant **Sarah Gurman**

Production Director **Chris Hemesath**
Production Manager **Michelle Duggan**
Colour Manager **Teri Bell**

A WELDON OWEN PRODUCTION
Copyright © 2008 Weldon Owen Inc.

ISBN: 978-1-905825-53-0

10 9 8 7 6 5 4 3 2 1

Printed in China.

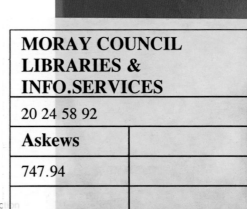

contents

the power of colour

Many people proclaim how much they "love colour", and what they
likely mean is that they're not afraid to use lots of colour in their lives.
For others, colour can seem daunting, whether for whole walls or a
few small cushions. There's no shame in being intimidated by bold
colours—a trip to the d.i.y. shop, with hundreds of colours in minutely
varying shades, can overwhelm even a secure colour fan.

When you're looking for a new palette or just one bold hue to
perk up a space, it's a good idea to consult a colour wheel, like the
one to the right. Notice that the colours on the right of the wheel,
featuring yellows, oranges, and reds, have warm undertones. The
left half—with its purples, blues, and greens—consists of colours that
are cool. Use these underlying "temperatures" to your advantage
when decorating. If you're looking for a refreshing space, choose
a cool colour. If you want a glowing room, select a warm hue.

Also consider the tried-and-tested methods that designers
use to arrive at successful colour combinations. Colours that are
neighbours on the wheel, such as greens, yellows, and oranges,
automatically look at home as a group. Complementaries are hues
that sit directly across from each other on the wheel, such as blue

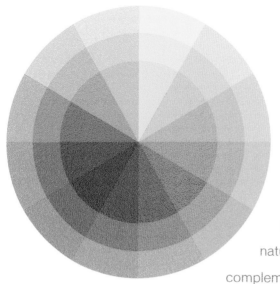

tool of the trade

Take the guesswork out of choosing a palette by using a colour wheel, which maps the relationships between colours. As the pros know, those are the key to mixing colours successfully.

and orange. By nature of their contrast, complementaries make each other appear more intense when paired. For that reason, a colour is often used with a lighter (or darker) shade of its complementary, rather than both colours at equal saturation.

Lastly, don't forget about the impact of black. Technically the absence of colour, black absorbs all hues in the spectrum and reflects none of them. It is the perfect backdrop for an eye-catching piece of furniture, it pairs beautifully with every colour, and it instantly adds drama and sophistication to any space.

This book is filled with inspiration, ideas and tips for using colours boldly. If finding a perfect palette seems a challenge, relax and enjoy the process. Once you've found it, the result will reward the effort.

blues

Cobalt, cornflower, royal blue, turquoise—if blue is your favourite colour, you're far from alone. It's an easy colour to love, and easily the most popular colour in the rainbow. In a dining room or bedroom—and whatever the shade—blue will always be in style.

using blue

Cool and calming, blue is a tried-and-tested classic. It's a soothing shade that can be used to create a tranquil oasis, open up a room or give your office a crisp look.

starry night

The relaxing nature of blue makes it a suitable choice for a bedroom. Many strong colours feel too vibrant for sleeping, but even the brightest cobalt or peacock blue can be simultaneously powerful and soothing.

cooling effects

Evocative of oceans, blue is also a fitting choice for a bathroom. Take care to select a shade that's not too pale, or the space might seem chilly. Wood elements will warm it up and balance out any white porcelain.

far and away

Blue is a receding colour, meaning it looks farther away than it is. Painting the walls blue is a quick way to make a small space feel larger. Light blue ceilings suggest the sky and can also help make a room feel taller.

true colours

A blue room lit with harsh blue-white lights or green fluorescents can feel a bit like an institutional space. Warm up your blues by using incandescent bulbs in fixtures or by lighting candles to balance out the electric lights.

endless options

Blue looks terrific with essentially every colour in the rainbow—think of the versatility of a pair of blue jeans. Anything you'd pair denim with, from deepest red to golden yellow to pure green, will look just as good in your rooms.

loyal blue

Have you ever wondered why politicians wear navy blue suits? Deep blue is associated with honesty and loyalty, which makes it an excellent choice for a home office or for any space where you'll be hosting potential clients.

stay awhile In a dining area, selecting welcoming shades of blue will encourage guests to pull up a chair, make themselves comfortable and stay beyond dessert.

earth and sea

Chocolate brown and shades of turquoise are an increasingly popular combination. Mix like textures, such as a velvet couch and velvety walls (left), or similar patterns (right).

the perfect pair As seen in traditional delftware (above), rich blue is timeless when paired with crisp white. A glossy white ceiling counters this blue's duskiness.

viva aqua Covering surfaces with vibrant blue tiles–whether in a kitchen or a bathroom–is a bold way to bring the shimmering quality of the sea to an indoor spot.

great lengths

A lapis storage wall running the length of this classical hallway makes a dramatic architectural statement.

wood accents add warmth to an expanse of bold colour

Stainless steel plays up the coolness of navy blue, while a teak stool and box shelving, along with woven rattan bins, are earthy complements. Paler blue jars provide an accent colour, and white towels pop against this serene, spa-like backdrop.

mix and match

Botanical prints feel modern
when mixed with clean-lined
furnishings. Choose fabrics
or wallpapers in bright colours
to inject some personality into
a small space. Pair them with
softer tones for balance.

look on the upside The brilliant blue ceiling of this rustic room draws the eye upwards. The rug, chairs, artwork and other accent pieces echo the ceiling's hue.

oranges

A spot of orange is instantly energising—just think about the feeling a fiery sunset or a ripe mango can evoke. If you want to breathe a little life into any room of the house that's feeling a bit drab, you can't go wrong with accent pieces—or full walls—in this vibrant hue.

using orange

Orange is energetic but can also come across as candy-coloured. To counter that effect, use nuanced shades and pair them with softer colours.

lasting effects

Orange has a tendency to cycle in and out of fashion. Skirt the trends by selecting shades that are somewhat more complex, such as coral, tangerine or terracotta, and you're likely to enjoy them for a longer period.

the peach pit

It's a common mistake to try to "tone down" a bright colour by adding white to the paint, which tends to result in timid pastels. In the case of orange, you'll wind up with peach. So pick a shade and stick with it.

good sport

For a powerful palette, pair orange with blue, its complementary. To avoid the look of a sports team's clubhouse, consider variations on both colours: tangerine with periwinkle or deep persimmon with navy.

what a bargain

In advertising colour theory, orange signals an inexpensive option: think fast-food chains and rental-car companies. Anything that is cheap plastic or at all poorly made could seem even chintzier in orange.

trial size

Orange can be a big commitment. Try using the colour in a small space such as a guest toilet or on a focal wall, rather than over an entire room. Once you're used to it, it's easy enough to add more orange.

extra spicy

In a kitchen or dining room, true orange can feel a bit saccharine. A better background for meals are spicier shades, such as paprika, cumin or saffron, which will enhance a meal rather than overwhelm it.

traveller's retreat Not for the shy and retiring, this bedroom gets its global flair from orange walls and tasselled silk lanterns, paired with a steamer trunk and globe.

all things equal

Bold accessories–a papaya
mohair throw and cushions,
turquoise goblets–look
sharp against a zebra print.

framing nature Taking colour cues from autumn leaves and dried botanicals, this well-appointed outdoor living room feels as warm and welcoming as a campfire.

38

eastern spice

From the warmest part of the colour wheel come orange, red and pink—combined here to create a sensual setting. Sheer panels delineate a sleeping space and add style.

orange pop Feature just one orange element—a long, streamlined sofa or lacquered table—against a white background to add instant playfulness to a room.

purples

Depending on a purple's balance of red and blue, it can appear warm or cool. Many people associate purple with royalty, but it's also linked to creativity. Use bright purple to inspire and motivate. Consider soft lavender when you want a wonderfully tranquil effect.

using purple

You don't have to be a king or queen to surround yourself with this royal hue. Use it to add richness to a room, or to give candlelight some added drama.

go for baroque

Though subject to trends in most arenas, interior designers have used the complementary pairing of regal purple and metallic gold since Renaissance times. Go for a Baroque look by employing this duo in your home.

tranquility now

Heralded as a colour with restorative properties, purple is the perfect hue to use in a luxury spa bath or a dressing room. Add towels and other linens in a cooler tint (or tints) of lavender to create a calm, contemplative mood.

wine notes

Warm purples look great by candlelight. Select a powerful shade of plum, aubergine or cabernet for a dining room, living room or bedroom–or anywhere there will be candles adding to an evening's festivities.

return of deco

For a daring yet classic palette, think about the colours of the Art Deco period. One after another, aubergine, cranberry, teal and gold have come back onto the catwalks, and the home design arena is sure to follow suit.

last not least

Violet, which lands at the extreme end of the colour spectrum, can be a hard colour to categorise. A shade of violet with a bit more blue to it creates an ethereal backdrop in any low-lit space, where it can't be easily identified.

purple reign

Purple's renewed and growing popularity has it popping up in unlikely spots–from kitchen appliances to bathroom fixtures and fabrics, to name just a few. As a result, purple now seems at home in any room.

friendly neighbours With combinations of magenta, purple and indigo, these bedrooms demonstrate the innate harmony of hues adjacent on the colour wheel.

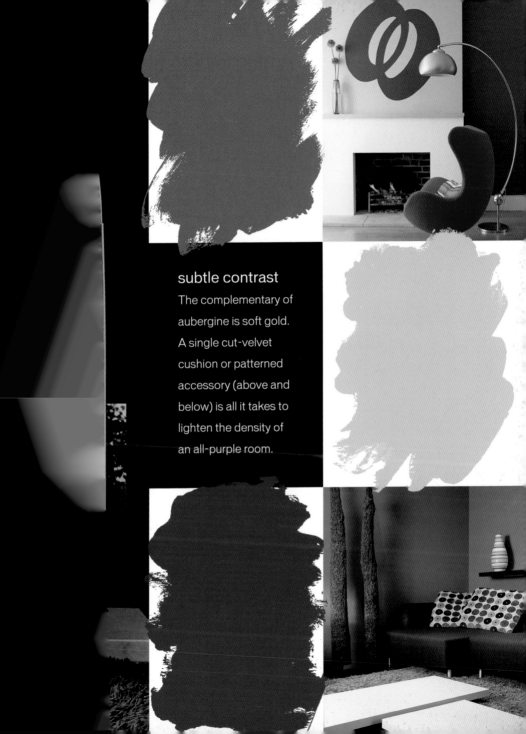

subtle contrast

The complementary of aubergine is soft gold. A single cut-velvet cushion or patterned accessory (above and below) is all it takes to lighten the density of an all-purple room.

seat of power Unexpected purple embellishments, such as the fringed silk cushions on these mid-century chairs, are an elegant touch in a neutral space.

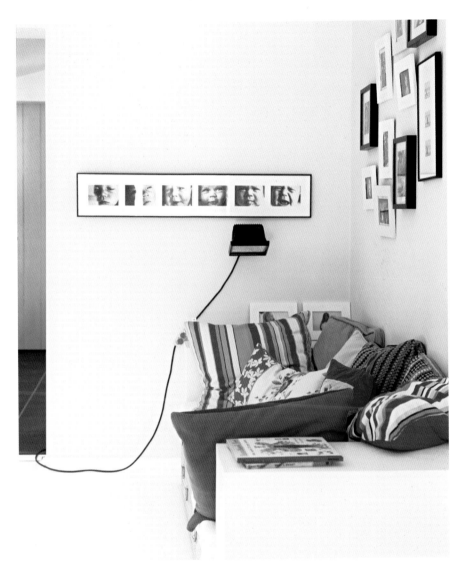

the antineutral Red-purple looks even more vibrant behind cool stainless steel and warm wood. In a mix of patterns, it's equally at home in an all-white setting.

soft shading

Multiple tints of a hue have natural harmony, as seen in this dining room. Earthy elements balance out such bold strokes as lilac lights and modern chairs re-covered in lavender.

graphic designs

Saturated red and violet are
an energetic pairing. Choose
neutral colours and natural
materials to tone down the
vibrancy, or go all the way
with modern chairs, oversize
prints and plastic accents.

exploring space Used broadly, dark plum almost magically recedes into the background, making pure white objects and interesting textures look more vivid.

yellows

Shades of yellow convey warmth and optimism, as they mimic the vital nature of sunshine. That's why yellow is so often described as "cheerful". Capitalise on the colour's positive effects by sprinkling it generously throughout the house, or go all out in a single room.

using yellow

The only colour whose brightness increases as it gets more saturated, yellow is fun to experiment with. Use it for dramatic effects or to add a hint of gentle cheer.

abandon caution

Many caution signs are made in bright yellow and contrasting black so that they'll be spotted easily. Employ this eye-catching strategy and combine the two in any room that you want to ensure will never be overlooked.

here comes the sun

A sunny yellow bedroom can brighten the mood of a dreary day, but pick a shade that isn't overly saturated: bright yellow may feel overwhelming on a sunny morning and could make it hard to wind down at night.

neutral whites

Warm yellows look great combined with pure white in a kitchen. White can also help neutralise the yellow, which was shown in at least one study to promote more arguments than any other colour when used on walls.

bright lights

Yellow, like other warm colours, will turn greenish under fluorescent lighting and look peachy under rosy incandescents. To get the truest rendering of your selected shade of yellow, you'll want to opt for full-spectrum lighting.

primary school

Yellow looks great as part of a citrusy palette (that is, with orange and lime) or as an accent for brown or grey. The trio of primary colours—yellow, red and blue—will evoke a kids' playroom, whether or not that's your aim.

power of purple

Yellow's complementary is purple, so if a canary yellow chair isn't as wild as you'd expected, toss in an aubergine pillow. From pale lavender to deep plum, accents of purple will up the intensity of any shade of yellow.

sunny disposition This ultra-contemporary, stainless-steel kitchen would feel plainly industrial without its quirky yellow walls and ceiling, and its accents of red.

a welcome note

Sunflower yellow walls
make a clear statement in
an entryway: the vibe of this
house is bright and breezy.

fresh picked Lemon yellow looks especially harmonious with lime green. Use the two in matched saturation and equal amounts to make the most of the pairing.

sun salutation

All-over yellow mosaic tiles
blur the boundaries of this
small bath and set off sleek
fixtures in pristine porcelain.

time and again Golden yellow is a surprisingly timeless hue. Notice how this antique table and vintage shawl-style tablecloth add vibrancy to these rooms.

bend the rules

The boldest statements are often the result of flouting tradition. Here the duo of red and yellow—considered a faux pas by many—is used unapologetically. The black wall intensifies the palette.

easy choice Yellow is bold without being overbearing. When incorporating another primary, such as blue, use softened shades, to avoid a playhouse look.

reds

You can't go wrong with red—it's practically the neutral of the bold colour palette. Suitable for even the most traditional styles, red declares confidence and sophistication. A bold sweep of crimson on any surface is the fastest way to make a statement.

using red

Never underestimate the power of red. As long as you don't let it overpower you or your rooms, it's a great choice for perking up traditional and modern decors.

hot stuff

An advancing colour—one that reaches the human eye faster than other colours—red can make a room smaller. Red is also a hot colour, so be sure to choose a space big enough and cool enough to handle it.

season's greetings

When using red with its complementary, green, it's better not to use both at full saturation—you'll wind up with a room that begs a Christmas tree. To give red the starring role, use a muted grey-green such as sage or moss.

exotic locale

Pairing red with either hot pink or orange has long been a no-no. But a palette of all three—red, pink and orange—has recently come into vogue. Set against warm wood tones, it evokes tropical getaways or the Far East.

perfect match

Anything but the truest red will have either a little bit of orange or purple in it. Placed side by side, these minor variations will be amplified. So choose a shade of red you like and keep a swatch handy for matching purposes.

rosy glow

All bright colours will cast a reflection on anything near them—in red's case, it's pink. So keep that in mind when planning a red-painted room: as soon as you turn on the lights, everything will take on a rosy appearance.

modern red

Accents of red give life to a modern, minimalist space. Red goes well with almost any building material—from steel to wood to concrete—yet holds its own in the presence of even the boldest architecture.

common thread

An intense colour such as fire-engine red can tie differing spaces together, as seen with the wall, stools, throw and cushions in this lofty, mixed-use room.

repeat appearance Take advantage of red's appetite-inducing properties by using it in a dining room or kitchen. Rows of chairs or glasses multiply the impact.

sleep patterns

Red and white is an arresting combination. Make the classic look your own by mixing patterns, such as toile, wide stripes, gingham and assorted checks.

red-handed Flowers, paintings and prints in your favourite crimson hue can enliven an otherwise neutral room (left) or add impact to an already bold space.

everyday red

If you love red but want a warmer look, choose a softer shade for walls—such as brick red or deep cinnabar—combine it with wood and pick true-red accessories.

centre of attention Red is so eye-catching that any note will always stand out. Paired with avocado in a mainly black-and-white room, this red chair is the star.

take notice

Make a statement with
bright custom bathroom
fixtures such as this racing-
car red bath and sink.

seeing red Shallow red lacquer cabinets seem to pop right out of their wood and glass surround, as does a red car in a Cuban street-scene photograph.

greens

From shocking chartreuse to the earthiest olive, green is accessible and complex at the same time. As green has more variations visible to the human eye than any other colour, picking just the right shade of it can be a challenge—but then again, why limit yourself to one?

using green

The friendly spirit of green makes it ideal for shared spaces. Whether you're evoking nature or adding get-up-and-go accents, it's good to be green.

swatch watch

The spectrum of greens runs from teal at the blue end to chartreuse at the yellow end, which can make it tricky to shop for things that match. Keep a swatch with you, because your "pistachio" may be another person's "lime".

natural selections

When using green and red together, picture a bouquet of cut flowers. Red tulips in a bunch will be roughly one-quarter red and the rest green. Following this ratio can lend your scheme the right amount of punch.

accessibly bold

Unlike most other colours, where bold often means bright, green offers a wealth of approachable shades. If you want to make a bold statement but are intimidated by the likes of coral and violet, try a wall of vivid olive.

great outdoors

Use green anywhere you want the clean feeling of the outdoors. A tonal palette of various shades of green—keep it to no more than five—can make even a room with limited windows feel like an indoor-outdoor space.

green light

Green means go, so use it anywhere you need a call to action, such as a home office or utility room. To maximise the effect, choose an apple, lime or any other bright shade that strikes you as inspiring and motivating.

in good health

Grassy green has gained a new connotation in recent years, through its use in packaging and ad campaigns to indicate healthy or earth-friendly choices. It's a statement that will translate to any room you apply it to.

balancing act Jade green is a good candidate for a complementary colour scheme. Here, it's used lavishly enough to balance out even the boldest of reds.

private rain forest

Nature's influence is evident in this inviting bathroom, where the leafy-green tiled shower is complemented by terracotta floor tiles. Sand-coloured Venetian plaster on the walls adds to the room's earthiness.

floral notes A tip from the flower market: chocolate cosmos suggest a bright and unexpected colour combination—lime green with gold and deepest purple.

attention grabber Use a colour like grass green to highlight features that might go unnoticed, such as shelves backed by chartreuse or interior shutters.

wall candy

If you love colour and can't pick just one, select a few favourites and use them broadly on neighbouring walls. Punctuate them with graphic artwork in equally vibrant hues.

along the grain

Typical of the California Arts
and Crafts style is this mix of
grey-green and warm woods.
Originally inspired by a forest
of redwoods, it's a look that's
right at home with indoor
greenery and outdoor views.

pinks

It takes a courageous soul to love hot pink, and an even more courageous one to decorate with it. Sure, it's traditionally associated with girlishness—sugar and spice and everything nice—but if you're in touch with your playful side, and ready to show it off, pink is for you.

using pink

Everyone looks good in pink—though few realise it—
so don't let the doubters faze you. Since pink can work
in just about any room, you'll be sitting pretty in no time.

palatable pink

Be careful to choose the
right pink for the function
of a space. In a dining
area, bubble-gum pink
may seem unappealing.
Try matching the shade
of something you might
serve—a chilled borscht
or a raspberry sorbet.

nurturing nature

In a bedroom, pinks are
especially flattering.
When decorating a room
for a child, go all out with
a mix of pink and purple.
In an elegant space for
grown-ups, pair magenta
with grey, or soft pink
with an earthy green.

one-hit wonder

Sometimes a single item
in hot pink—a vibrant
velvet chair or a mohair
throw—in an otherwise
neutral space is enough
to increase the colour
quotient. Even in small
doses, pink can make
a powerful statement.

opposites attract

Lime green sits directly
across from pink on the
colour wheel, and, unlike
so many complementary
combinations, they make
a popular duo. Use both
hues at full saturation
to conjure up springtime
or classic preppy flair.

petal soft

Flowery pink is an ideal
choice for a bathroom,
where it's charming while
also seeming to be softly
scented. Alternatively, a
warmer reddish pink can
be soothing when you
step out of the shower on
a cold winter's morning.

femme fatale

For those who fear the
connotations of "pink,"
take refuge in the names.
Steer clear of anything
described as "rose" or
"petal", and opt for more
complex and elegant
choices, such as "coral",
"salmon" and "zinnia".

back in time

Candy floss pink is a colour
that almost unavoidably
suggests 1950s nostalgia.
Pairing it with cherry red
accents or modern acrylic
furnishings can give that nod
to the past a playful twist.

pop art As complementaries, green and pink can be paired in a variety of ways. Here, the colours of cherry blossoms and jade support an Asian-inspired theme.

new traditions

Prove that even the most traditional homes can have a sense of humour by combining daring shades of hot pink, magenta and purple in an otherwise classic bathroom.

exercising control To keep fuchsia from feeling too over-the-top, use it in controlled doses—a pattern or piece of art—in an otherwise black-and-white space.

blacks

Beige, sage and chocolate
have ruled the design world
for so long that black and
grey can seem like daring
choices. Conventional
wisdom says every room
needs something black, but
rooms that fully embrace
this anticolour might just
be the boldest of them all.

using black

Many people who aren't timid about wearing black shy away from decorating with it. Used wisely, shades of black can add depth and drama to your decor.

to the touch

Working with muted colours provides the perfect opportunity to go bold with texture and pattern. If embossed wall finishes, embroidered fabric or faux fur seems too loud for you, consider them in a soft black.

shining star

White reflects light, while black absorbs it. You can counter this darkening effect by incorporating shiny surfaces—such as high-gloss paint, laminate and leather—into a room to keep the space from getting gloomy.

stark contrast

Freshen up black or grey with pure white. (Pure white can be difficult to find, as most whites have undertones of either blue or yellow.) For a quieter but still stylish contrast, try pairing charcoal grey with the palest ivory.

depth of character

To the human eye, dark grey seems to have more depth to it than any other colour. Capitalise on that character trait in a small room by painting walls grey—or a colour with lots of grey in it—to make the space feel larger.

test patch

Black and grey, each a blend of many colours, may appear to be dark shades of other colours in differing light. When painting walls, paint a test square and observe it at various times of the day, under different lighting.

traditional twist

Ditching its association with the industrial-chic furnishings of the 1980s, black is now being used by cutting-edge designers to update the look of classic pieces, such as a French Country armchair or a Louis XVI chest.

studied minimalism

In a predominantly white room with lofty ceilings, French doors and ample windows, black acts as a point of reference. The giant tufted ottoman, black furniture legs and ebonised wood floors work in tandem to ground the space. The gilt accents, spare sofa and oversize mirror keep the room light and bright.

high contrast Enhance the impact of a graphic black-and-white pattern with a spot of contrast—a pink blanket or an earthenware vase and branches of greenery.

set a scene

Nothing could show off the curvaceousness of these vintage-inspired porcelain fixtures quite like black.

rethinking grey

The truest neutral, medium grey gracefully balances a bright shade like goldenrod. The grey's softness takes the edge off the pulsating yellow while highlighting it at the same time.

stone age

The variegated tile covering the surfaces of this bathroom showcases the subtle variations of black, grey and silver found in a slab of stone.